Big Brown Bat

Rick Chrustowski

Henry Holt and Company ◆ New York

Henry Holt and Company, LLC, *Publishers since 1866*
175 Fifth Avenue, New York, New York 10010 |www.HenryHoltKids.com|

Henry Holt® is a registered trademark of Henry Holt and Company, LLC.
Copyright © 2008 by Rick Chrustowski
All rights reserved. Distributed in Canada by H. B. Fenn and Company Ltd.

Library of Congress Cataloging-in-Publication Data
Chrustowski, Rick.
Big brown bat / Rick Chrustowski.—1st ed.
p.   cm.
ISBN-13: 978-0-8050-7499-4 / ISBN-10: 0-8050-7499-6
1. Big brown bat—Juvenile literature.   I. Title.
QL737.C595C47 2008   599.4'7—dc22   2007040032

First Edition—2008 / Designed by Véronique Lefèvre Sweet
The artist used up to forty layers of colored pencil over watercolor wash
on 140-pound watercolor paper to create the illustrations for this book.
Printed in China on acid-free paper. ∞

1   3   5   7   9   10   8   6   4   2

For Betty

*S*hadows reach across fields one evening in June. As the warm glow of sunset fades, butterflies and songbirds settle in to sleep. Now the sky belongs to night creatures.

Big brown bats wake up in their secret roost. They live up in the rafters of a farmhouse attic. The room is dark and quiet like a cave. But this cave is hot and dry—the perfect place for a nursery.

The bats rush off on their nightly hunt. They stretch
their wings and drop into the air one by one. Flapping and
circling around an air vent, the bats squeeze through the
narrow slats to the outside world.

One bat stays behind. She hooks her thumb claws into a rafter and hangs down. Soon she gives birth to a wrinkly pink bat pup. She cradles him in her tail apron and licks him clean.

The pup can't see yet, but he can hold on. He snuggles under his mother's wing and drinks the warm milk she makes for him.

A few nights later the mother bat leaves her pup alone while she hunts. He clings to the rafter upside down and calls for her to return. His squeaking cries echo through the darkness.

Finally at dawn, she returns to feed him. The pup grabs on to her fur and purrs himself to sleep like a kitten.

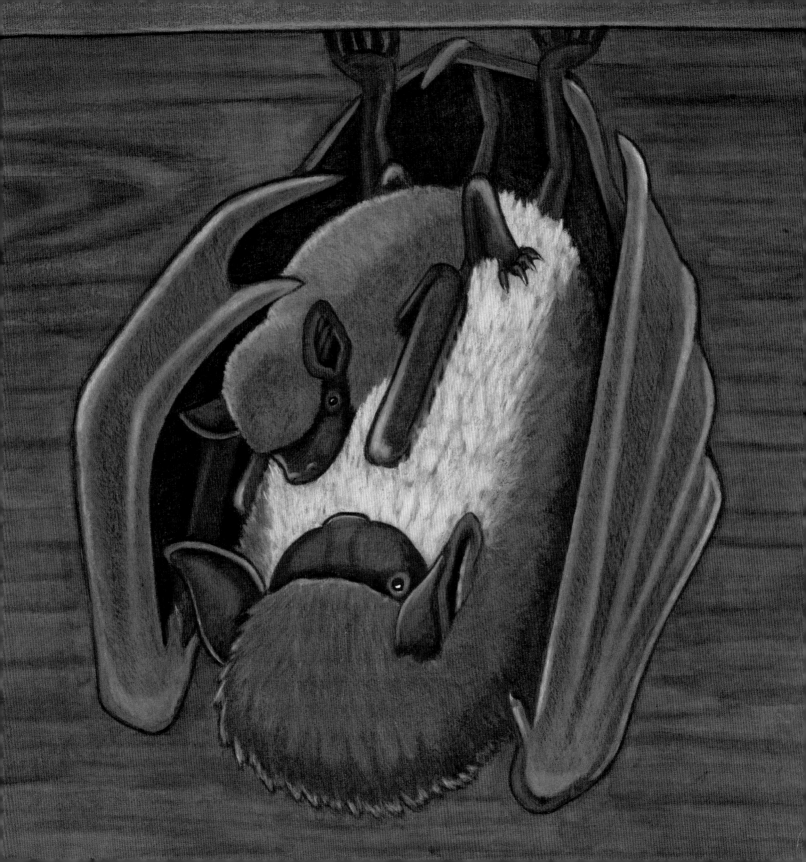

Over the next week, the other bats have babies. While they hunt, their babies stay close together to keep warm. The oldest pup dangles from the rafter and pumps his wings for practice. He is almost strong enough to fly.

When the pup is three weeks
old he lets go of the rafter and
plunges into darkness. *Whoosh!* His
wings flash open and catch the air.
The young bat flies with his hands. His long fingers
and short arms are wrapped between two layers of
rubbery skin. When he spreads his fingers, his wings
open wide. He pumps the air to dash forward. *Loop.*
Swoop. Spin. He flips in midair
and tries to snag the rafter
with his toe claws. After
lots of fluttery stumbling,
he finally grabs hold.

One week later the mother bat weans the pup off her milk. He is a young bat now and needs to hunt for his supper. He follows his mother out the air vent and gets his first look at the vast starry sky.

Just then his mother zips by, chasing a June bug. The bat leaps off the building and soars after her. He watches her swoop down on the beetle and scoop it up in her tail apron.

Like his mother, the young bat uses his ears when hunting. As he flies he opens his mouth and shrieks into the darkness. The pulses of sound spread like ripples on water. They bounce off objects and return to his ears as echoes. The bat gets clues from each echo; together, they create a snapshot of the world around him: trees, houses, other bats.

An insect is flapping its wings up there in the treetop. It has skinny legs . . . long antennae . . . it's a moth!

The bat pinpoints his prey. He shrieks faster, 30 pulses per second, 50, now 75. The echoes return at a furious pace.

The moth has a secret weapon. She can hear the bat shrieks with a pair of ears on her back. She dodges left, whirls upward, then swerves right. But the bat flies straight and cuts her off.

Just before the bat attacks
he shrieks 200 times per
second. The echoes are so
close together they return
as a buzz of information.
He rushes in for the kill.

The moth has one last
chance to escape. She folds
up her wings and dives from
the sky like a fighter plane,
just out of reach.

The bat doesn't go hungry for long. He learns quickly that a June bug is easier to catch than an underwing moth. He bites through the beetle's armor and tastes his first insect meal. After a week the bat is a hunting machine, gobbling up one half of his own weight in insects each night.

In July the bat eats cucumber beetles, in August he eats leafhoppers, and in September he hunts for green stinkbugs.

By fall the bat is fully grown and padded up with extra weight. The stored fat will keep him alive through winter. Cold nights and hard freezes tell the bats that it's time to leave the attic.

The bat follows his mother across farm fields and down a ravine where limestone cliffs hide secret caves. He skims one last drink from the river, then disappears into the hideaway.

During the icy winter, the bat clings to the face of a stone wall. For six months, while he hibernates, blood barely flows through his veins. Some days his body temperature falls below freezing. He's still alive, just waiting for spring.

When the snow finally melts and insects buzz through the field, the bat and his family will wake up and own the night sky once again.

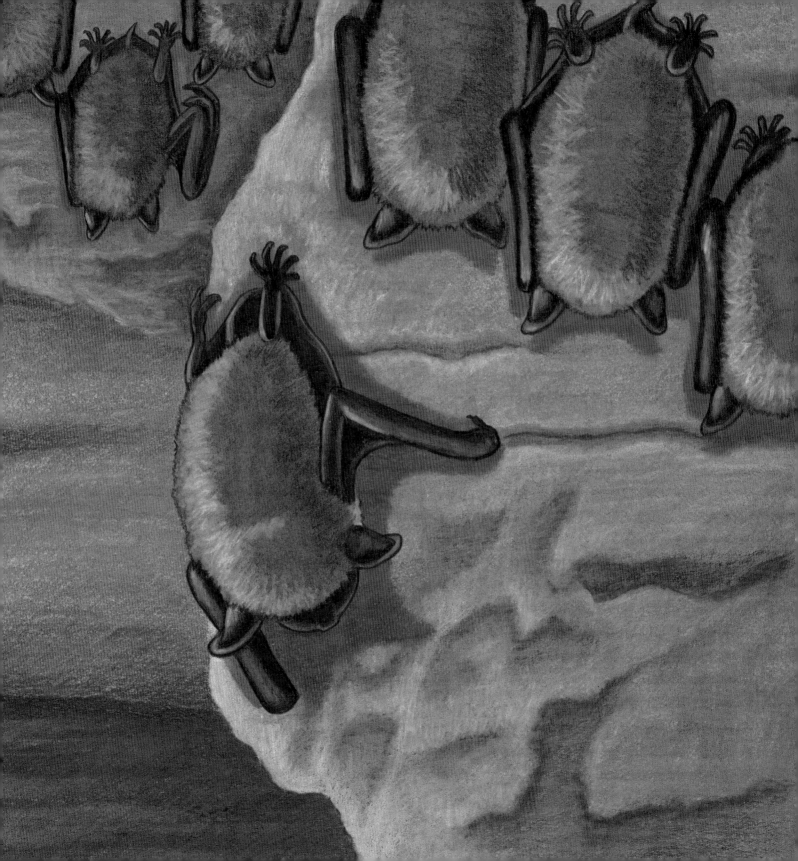

Bat Basics

Look into the sky on a warm summer night. A winged shadow might dash overhead. Maybe it's a bat tracking its prey!

Bats are mammals: They are warm-blooded, their bodies are covered with hair, and they give birth to live young that feed on their mother's milk. Bats are the only mammals that can fly.

There are around 1,000 different bat species in the world. Of the 40 species that live in the Western Hemisphere, big browns are one of the most common. They can be found from central Canada through the United States and into South America.

A big brown bat isn't as big as its name suggests. It weighs a half ounce and its body is 5 inches long with a 10-inch wingspan; it's about the size of a songbird. Because its wings are also hands, it has incredible control in flight. It can hover like a hummingbird, zip forward and back like a dragonfly, and flip in the air like an acrobat.

When a big brown bat flies with its mouth open it is using echolocation. The sound pulses it makes cannot be heard by humans. By listening closely to the echoes that return, a bat can tell if an insect is a moth or a beetle, how far away it is, how high off the ground, how fast it is moving, and even the texture of its body. A bat can eat one half or more of its own weight in insects each night.

Early in summer, female big browns gather in small maternity roosts in barns, abandoned buildings, and houses to give birth. Their pups suckle for the next month and then they are ready to fly and hunt for their own food.

With a little luck a big brown bat can live to be 18 or 19 years old. But most scientists believe a 10-year lifespan is more likely.

For more information about bats of all kinds, visit Bat Conservation International at their Web site: www.batcon.org.